THE OFFICIAL  RSPCA PET GUIDE

Care for Your

Tropical Fish

CONTENTS

Record card	4
Introduction	5
Freshwater fish in the tropics	6
Biology	8
Fish for the aquarium	10
Stocking your aquarium	18
Aquaria	22
Tank decoration and water quality	26
Aquarium equipment	28
Water plants	30
Fitting out an aquarium	32
Home aquarium checklist	33
Picking out healthy stock	34
The healthy tropical fish	36
Settling in your fish	37
Feeding	38
Maintenance and handling	40
Ailments	42
Reproduction	44
Your questions answered	46
Index	48

First published in 1986 by
William Collins Sons & Co Ltd, London
New edition published in 1990

Reprinted by
HarperCollins*Publishers*
77-85 Fulham Palace Road
Hammersmith
London W6 8JB

The HarperCollins website address is
www.**fire**and**water**.com

07 06 05 04 03 02 01
18 17 16 15 14 13 12

This is a fully revised and extended edition of *Care for your Tropical Fish*,
first published in 1986

© Royal Society for the Prevention of Cruelty to Animals 1986, 1990

Text of the 1986 edition by M. Richardson; text revisions and additions
for this edition by Dick Mills

Designed and edited by The Templar Company plc
Pippbrook Mill, London Road, Dorking, Surrey RH4 1JE

Front cover photograph: Animal Ark, London
Text photographs: D. Allison, Heather Angel, Bruce Coleman Ltd,
Dick Mills, Mike Sandford, Spectrum Colour Library Ltd

Illustrations: Simon Burr/David Lewis Artists and
Robert Morton/Bernard Thornton Artists

**A catalogue record for this book is available
from the British Library**

ISBN 0 00 412548 7

Printed by Midas Printing Ltd, Hong Kong

First things first, animals are fun. Anybody who has ever enjoyed the company of a pet knows well enough just how strong the bond between human and animal can be. Elderly or lonely people often depend on a pet for their only company, and this can be a rewarding relationship for both human and animal. Doctors have proved that animals can be instrumental in the prevention of and recovery from mental or physical disease. Children learn the meaning of loyalty, unselfishness and friendship by growing up with animals.

But the commitment to an animal doesn't begin and end with a visit to the local pet shop. A pet should never be given as a 'surprise' present. The decision to bring a pet into your home should always be discussed and agreed by all the members of your family. Bear in mind that parents are ultimately responsible for the health and well-being of the animal for the whole of its lifetime. If you are not prepared for the inevitable expense, time, patience and occasional frustration involved, then the RSPCA would much rather that you didn't have a pet.

Armed with the facts, aware of the pitfalls but still confident of your ability to give a pet a good home, the next step is to find where you can get an animal from. Seek the advice of a veterinary surgeon or RSPCA Inspector about reputable local breeders or suppliers. Do consider the possibility of offering a home to an animal from an RSPCA establishment. There are no animals more deserving of loving owners.

As for the care of your pet, you should find in this book all you need to know to keep it happy, healthy and rewarding for many years to come. Responsible ownership means happy pets. Enjoy the experience!

Terence C. Bate

TERENCE BATE BVSc, LLB, MRCVS
Chief Veterinary Officer, RSPCA

Record card

Record sheet for your own aquarium

(photograph or portrait)

Species _____

Feeding notes _____

_____

_____

_____

_____

_____

Plant varieties _____

_____

_____

_____

_____

_____

_____

Date acquired _____

Medical notes _____

Disease diagnosed _____

Treatment used _____

Fish isolated/or not _____

Successful/unsuccessful _____

_____

Breeding record _____

Variety/generation _____

Best characteristics _____

Date conditioned _____

Date put together _____

Date eggs hatched _____

Foods given _____

Number of fish raised _____

Veterinary surgeon's name _____

Practice address _____

_____

Surgery hours _____

_____

Tel. no. _____

Introduction

The first public aquarium in the world was opened in England in 1852, in the Zoological Gardens in Regent's Park, London, and since then, keeping and breeding tropical fish has increased in popularity enormously.

Tropical fish can be divided into two categories: freshwater and marine fish. This book is concerned only with freshwater tropical fish. The requirements for marine fish tend to be complex and demand considerable expertise, as well as more time, effort and money than the newcomer to fish keeping will wish to expend.

That said, keeping freshwater fish as pets still requires certain basic commitments on the part of the owner. Fish are living creatures and although they cannot show their feelings as demonstratively as cats or dogs, they still need to be well looked after if they are to thrive.

The black and silver stripes of the Angelfish and Black Widow Tetras complement each other and also provide a contrast to the bright colours of the Neon Tetras.

Many hundreds of brightly coloured tropical freshwater fish are readily available from aquarist shops. Time given to investigation and a little basic knowledge to ensure a congenial and healthy environment for your fish will make your aquarium a source of living interest and delight.

Freshwater fish in the tropics

Tropical freshwater fish come from many different habitats, ranging from the fast-flowing mountain streams of China to the huge inland freshwater lakes of Africa.

Most live-bearing fish such as Guppies, Swordtails, Platies and Mollies are native to the Central Americas, inhabiting waterways which often receive some tidal waters.

Colourful tetras are aquarium favourites; the diminutive Neon and Cardinal Tetras are closely related to the Piranha and share its South American watercourses along with other aquarium favourites, the Angelfish and Corydoras Catfish.

Slow-moving rivers of India and South-East Asia are the home of rasboras and barbs, whilst the graceful gouramis and belligerent Siamese Fighting Fish are able to survive often oxygen-depleted waters by virtue of their auxilliary breathing organs.

Both South America and Africa have their fair share of three other very popular, often specialized, groups of fishes – the cichlids, catfish and killifish.

Swamp

5. *Betta splendens*
6. *Colisa sota*
7. *Colisa fasciata*
8. *Otocinclus affinis*
9. *Corydoras julii*
10. *Corydoras aeneus*
11. *Ctenopoma nanum*

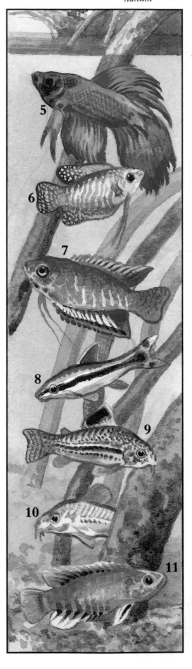

Rift Valley lake

1. *Melanochromis auratus*
2. *Pseudotropheus zebra*
3. *Hemichromis bimaculatus*
4. *Julidochromis ornatus*

Stream or river

12. *Paracheirodon innesi*
13. *Nematobrycon palmeri*
14. *Gasteropelecus atrigata*
15. *Gasteropelecus sternicla*
16. *Xiphophorus helleri*
17. *Barbus tetrazona*

18. *Brachydanio rerio*
19. *Poecilia reticulata*
20. *Hemigrammus ocellifer*
21. *Rasbora heteromorpha*
22. *Poecilia velifera*
23. *Poecilia mexicana*

24. *Botia macracantha*
25. *Pterophyclum scalare*
26. *Monodactylus argenteus*
27. *Anostomus anostomus*
28. *Labeo bicolor*

Biology

Scales Externally, the body of the fish is covered with small bony plates – scales – which are themselves covered with a delicate layer of skin (although this is usually too thin to be seen without a microscope) that enlarges the scales as the fish grows. On top of this is a layer of mucus with bactericidal properties. The scales can only protect the fish by growing. If the delicate skin is damaged, growth is affected, so the fish's well-being is put at risk. For this reason extreme care must be taken when handling fish – better still, try not to handle them at all if possible. If too much mucus is removed by handling, bacteria can get into the skin and set up an infection: if too much skin is removed, the scales cannot grow; if the scales cannot grow, the fish can lose body fluids or become infected and die.

Eyes Fish have no eyelids, so those kept in an aquarium need to be shaded from direct sunshine.

Gills Most fish breathe by taking in water through the mouth, which then closes, the muscles squeezing the water out through slits in the side of the throat. The bars between the slits are lined with delicate blood-filled filaments (gill filaments), which act like our lungs. They pick up oxygen from the water and remove the carbon dioxide from the fish's blood. The gills nestle below a large protective plate just behind the head, which is called the gill cover, or operculum.

Fins Fins are the most conspicuous features of a fish and are of great help in determining to which group of fish your specimen belongs. As well as having locomotory functions, they can serve other purposes, as described here.

Dorsal fin This fin may have spiny rays in front or may be made up entirely of soft rays. It acts as a keel to stabilize the fish and, if brightly marked, may be rather like a signalling flag, helping to keep shoals together. It can also be used to 'warn' other species.

Vertebra

Gill cover (operculum)

Intestine

Pectoral fins Just behind the operculum are the pectoral fins, which are the fish's equivalent of arms. Like the pelvic fins, they help the fish to brake and steer.

Pelvic fins The paired fins in front of the anal fin are the pelvic fins. These help with braking and steering.

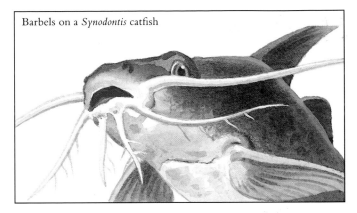

Barbels on a *Synodontis* catfish

Swim bladder Many fish (indeed most you are likely to encounter) have a large gas- or air-filled sac variously called the swim bladder, gas bladder or air bladder. This is not usually used for breathing, but acts as a buoyancy chamber to keep the fish at the required depth in the water without effort. The fish uses its swim bladder to make itself neutrally buoyant.

Muscle segment

Adipose fin Some fish (characins and catfish) have a small fatty fin called the adipose fin. No-one yet knows its precise function, but it will help you to identify an aquarium fish as a catfish or characin.

Barbels Some fish, notably bottom-dwelling species such as catfish and loaches, have 2–6 whiskery growths around the mouth; these 'barbels' are equipped with taste and touch cells, enabling the fish to locate food in dark, murky waters.

Caudal fin At the end of the body is the caudal or tail fin, which can be one of a variety of shapes. In the male swordtail the lower rays of the caudal fin are elongated into the colourful sword that gives these species their common name. The tail imparts the thrust of the side-to-side movements which make the fish go forwards.

Rib

Anal fin On the underside of the body, just behind the anus, is the anal fin. Like the dorsal fin, it acts as a stabilizer, except in the males of live-bearing species where it is used in reproduction. For example, in fish like Guppies, Swordtails, etc., the anal fin of the male is modified into a rod-like structure to transfer the sperm to the female.

Lateral line Running down the side of many fish is a line, called the lateral line, which is formed by a series of pores in a row of scales. The pores lead to a canal with pressure-sensitive organs. The lateral line system acts like a sense of 'distant touch', which can alert the fish to obstacles and dangers.

Fish for the aquarium

CHOOSING A SELECTION OF FISH

It's a good idea to choose a selection which live at varying depths (surface, middle-water and bottom levels), thereby maximizing all available tank space. To obtain both an aesthetic and 'ecological' balance, fish should be chosen to suit these areas although most, at some time or another, will visit areas other than those allocated to them.

To illustrate such a distribution, danios and rasboras are active surface area fish constantly on the move; the longer-finned Angelfish and gouramis are much slower in their movements, living happily in mid-water amongst the tall grassy plants accompanied by the decorative tetras and constantly foraging barbs. Bottom-dwelling fish, such as many catfish, are often nocturnal by nature and will spend the daytime hours (or when the tank is artificially lit) hidden among the rocks and plants waiting for 'night' to fall.

Live-bearing fish, although having upturned mouths of surface feeders, seem to occupy any level they feel like! We shall therefore describe these 'non-conformists' first.

THE GUPPY (*Poecilia reticulata*)

The many colourful strains of the Guppy are internationally recognized; its alternative common name of Millions Fish also confirms the fish's readiness to breed. The sexes are easily distinguished as the females, although much larger than the males, are less brightly patterned. The guppy is a shoaling fish and one of the most popular choices for the aquarium, being attractive, inexpensive and easy to keep.

THE SWORDTAIL (*Xiphophorus helleri*)

Green when found in the wild in Central America, this distinctive fish has been bred in red, black and many mixed colours. It grows to about 9 cm/3½ in long. The long extension to the bottom of the male's caudal fin makes the Swordtail instantly recognizable, but sex-reversal (female to male) is not uncommon in adult Swordtails.

Male Guppy (*Poecilia reticulata*)

Green Swordtail (*Xiphophorus helleri*)

Platy (*Xiphophorus maculatus*)

THE PLATY (*Xiphophorus maculatus*)
The platy is a peaceful, sociable fish which comes in a wide range of colours. Its preferred water temperature is probably 24°–26°C/75°–80°F and the aquarium should be well-lit to encourage algae growth. Platies can be reliable breeders.

THE MOLLY (*Poecilia* spp.)
These popular live-bearers can be green and gold spotted or all black, depending on which species you choose.

Include plenty of green matter in all live-bearers' diets.

Mollies (*Poecilia velifera*)

Surface feeders

All the fish found 'just under the surface' have a perfectly straight back, which allows their upturned mouths (ideal for scooping up floating foods, usually insects in nature) to get right up to the surface. Foods which float for some time are ideal for these fish.

ZEBRA DANIO (*Brachydanio rerio*)
A native of India, this fish enjoys a water temperature between 20° and 23°C/68° and 73°F. A very active and lively fish, it will reach a size of about 5 cm/2 in and is best kept in shoals. Females are much plumper than males. For novices, the Zebra Danio may be regarded as an ideal fish with which to begin breeding; the parents should be removed as soon as possible after spawning as they love eating their own eggs. Alternatively, use dense bunches of plants in which the eggs can lodge well out of their reach.

Zebra Danio (*Brachydanio rerio*)

GLASS CATFISH (*Kryptopterus bicirrhis*)
An almost transparent fish – you can see its bones – it has but a single ray for a dorsal fin (see p.27). It originates in South-East Asia, growing easily to about 10 cm/4 in long. It enjoys a temperature range of 21°–26°C/70°–80°F. As it is an active, free-swimming, shoaling fish don't keep just one, otherwise it may pine away. Unlike most other catfish it spends quite a time in the upper levels of the water.

Silver Hatchetfish (*Gasteropelecus sternicla*)

SILVER HATCHETFISH (*Gasteropelecus sternicla*)
The very deep body of this species from South America houses powerful muscles which 'flap' the pectoral fins as it leaps above the surface to chase insects or escape predators. A covered tank is very necessary for this family of fish if they are not to end up on the carpet! A peaceful shoaling species best kept in groups of six or more. They seem to prefer warmer water than most tropicals, within a range of 23–30°C/73–86°F.

SIAMESE FIGHTING FISH (*Betta splendens*)
This is a hardy fish, but you can only have one male in a tank otherwise fighting will break out. If you want to see it display, put a mirror at the side of the tank. When a female is present, the male fish blows a nest of bubbles under which to spawn and guard the floating eggs. Aquarium-cultivated strains usually have bodies and fins of one colour,

Siamese Fighting Fish (*Betta splendens*)

bright reds, blues and greens, but the 'Cambodia' Fighter (also aquarium-developed) has a cream body with coloured fins.

BUTTERFLY FISH (*Pantodon buchholzi*)
Inhabiting the Zaire region, the Butterfly Fish hangs motionless beneath the surface for long periods, waiting for insects to alight on the water. Like Hatchetfish, it can leap from the water to glide for some distance using its outspread pectoral fins, although it does not 'flap' them.

Incidentally, it is not until you look down on this fish from above the tank that you realize the significance of its common name – the pectoral fins are like butterfly wings. It is the only species in its genus and may be predatious towards small fishes.

Butterfly Fish (*Pantodon buchholzi*)

Midwater feeders

Easily identified by their terminal mouths situated right on the front of the snout, midwater swimmers form the largest group of fish and offer an almost limitless choice.

All are normal 'fish-shaped', with the dorsal and anal contours being similarly convex. The disc-shaped Angelfish and Discus are slower-moving fish, their narrow bodies enabling them to slip between plants effortlessly.

ANGELFISH (*Pterophyllum scalare*)
The disc-shaped body of the Angelfish is not representative of the cichlid family, but this South American fish is still an all-time aquarium favourite. The original wild species had a silver body with dark vertical bars, but there are now marbled, gold, albino and 'blushing' varietes with exaggerated fin lengths, all produced in the Far East by selective breeding. Angelfish make a graceful addition to the aquarium but, when large, may harass other smaller fish. Well-matched, self-selected pairs breed easily and look after their young.

CARDINAL TETRA (*Paracheirodon axelrodi*)
This brilliantly coloured fish from South America is not only related to the Piranha, but has just as many teeth. Similar in size (3cm/just over 1 in) to the Neon Tetra (*P. innesi*), the Cardinal is easily distinguishable – the Neon has only a half-length red band on the body.

GLOWLIGHT TETRA (*Hemigrammus erythrozonus*)
A delicately glowing red/gold line shines along the sides of the body and the top of the eye is red. This fish is seen at its best in a well-planted tank with a dark bottom covering.

Angelfish (*Pterophyllum scalare*)

Glowlight Tetra (*Hemigrammus erythrozonus*)

Harlequin Fish (*Rasbora heteromorpha*)

HARLEQUIN FISH (*Rasbora heteromorpha*)

A lively but peaceful rasbora which enjoys being in shoals, when all fish move as one. It will thrive on flaked fish food and grows to a size of about 4.5 cm/1¾ in and appreciates soft, acid water. It lays its eggs on the undersides of broad-leaved plants.

RUBY BARB (*Barbus nigrofasciatus*)

The Ruby Barb is so called because the colour of the male fish undergoes a remarkable change at breeding time. The whole body is suffused with rich red/purple, especially so in the head region; the female remains a dark-striped pale yellow fish. These barbs grow to about 5 cm/2 in and are very active fish. Supplement their flaked food with live food such as *Daphnia* and worms.

PEARL GOURAMI (*Trichogaster leeri*)

Very pretty fish, generally peaceful but sensitive to bad water conditions. Best kept in pairs, they reach a size of about 10 cm/4 in. They enjoy subdued light and build floating bubble nests in which they place their eggs.

TIGER BARB (*Barbus tetrazona*)

Growing to around 5 cm/2 in, this aquarium favourite from the Far East is easily recognized by its four dark bands and red-orange edges to the fins. If kept in small numbers, it may nip the fins of slower-moving fish but keeping a shoal may help solve this problem.

Pearl Gourami (*Trichogaster leeri*)

Tiger Barb (*Barbus tetrazona*)

Bottom-dwelling species

Not unexpectedly, bottom-swimming species have physical characteristics which are almost the opposite of surface-swimming fish. Their ventral (lower) contour is flat, allowing their mouths (often adorned with barbels) to get as near as possible to the bottom in order to search out and pick up food. A further reason for flat-bottomed bodies is so that the fish will not be lifted off the bottom by fast-flowing water currents and be swept away.

Some catfish, whilst not being entirely bottom-dwelling, have sucker-mouths for rasping off algae from rocks; the Chinese Sucking 'Loach' (*Gyrinocheilus aymonieri*) has a special hole in the upper gill cover in order to breathe to save releasing its 'sucker-hold' on the rock. (Incidentally, this fish is neither a loach nor does it come from China: to make matters worse it may attack other fish when adult.)

South America and Africa are excellent natural sources of large numbers of aquarium-suitable catfish and some aquarists specialize in these fish.

Many hobbyists tend to regard bottom-dwelling fish as scavengers, expecting them to thrive on food left over by other fish. While many catfish do obtain their food this way, they should not be denied food in their own right, and feeding fast-sinking, or tablet foods (especially last thing at night) will do much to ensure these fish get their rightful share of proper foods.

BRONZE CATFISH (*Corydoras aeneus*)

Catfish of this shoaling genus have no scales, their skin is covered by two rows of overlapping bony plates called scutes. Another characteristic physical feature is the ability to rotate each eye independently in the socket. An 'albino' form of this fish has been aquarium-developed.

PEPPERED CATFISH (*Corydoras paleatus*)

Like the preceding species, the Peppered Catfish is also a longstanding aquarium favourite.

Many corydoras are relatively easy to breed by the addition of some *cold* water to their aquarium. This simulates their natural conditions where melted ice-waters enter their South American river systems each spring and triggers breeding. During spawning, female corydoras carry the fertilized eggs between their pelvic fins to a hatching site, usually on plant leaves or the aquarium glass.

Pleco or Suckermouth Catfish (*Hypostomus plecostomus*)

Bronze Catfish (*Corydoras aeneus*)

PLECO (*Hypostomus plecostomus*)

Usually purchased for its algae-removing services, the Suckermouth Catfish or Pleco should continue to be given green foods once it has completed its allotted task, if it is to thrive. Vegetable matter forms a very essential part of its diet and the addition of lettuce, spinach leaves and green peas will be much appreciated.

Although a sunny tank location will encourage the growth of algae, the fish is not discomforted by any bright light; it can adjust the level of light entering its eye by expanding or contracting a lobe of skin over the pupil.

CLOWN LOACH (*Botia macracantha*)

This smart orange and black striped fish has very tiny scales, so much so that it appears to be naked. Under the eye it has an erectile spine which is usually raised in defence: watch out that it doesn't become lodged in the net when catching this very fast-moving fish – if you ever manage it! The Clown Loach is very 'sociable' and should be kept in small shoals. Fish in this genus (and other 'naked' species) may be irritated by chemicals used in remedies due to the skin being less protected than that of more 'scaly' species.

Clown Loach (*Botia macracantha*)

Stocking your aquarium

There are a great number of ways in which you can stock and furnish your aquarium. The vital things to remember are to choose fish that are mutually compatible, and not to overstock your tank. Three schemes are suggested here which would make a well–balanced aquarium and which would provide both a congenial environment for the fish and an attractive moving picture of colour and light. All the schemes listed below and opposite are based on a tank 60 × 38 × 30 cm/24 × 15 × 12 in.

SCHEME NO. 1

This is suitable for a tank in a hard and alkaline water area.

Fish
5 Tiger Barbs (*Barbus tetrazona*)
2 pairs Black Mollies (*Poecilia sphenops*)
2 pairs Guppies (*Poecilia reticulata*)
1 pair Swordtails (*Xiphophorus helleri*)
1 pair Pearl Gourami (*Trichogaster leeri*)
2-3 Corydoras (*Corydoras aeneus* or *paleatus*)
2 pairs Platies (*Xiphophorus maculatus*)
2 small Angelfish (*Pterophyllum scalare*)

Plants
Select plants of varying heights (with the tallest at the back and the shortest in the front). Approximately two dozen would be a good number, although this will depend on how much other tank decoration (rocks, stones, bogwood, etc.) you include. Choose from any of the plants listed below:
Echinodorus paniculatus (Amazon Swordplant)
Sagittaria
Vallisneria
Ludwigia (Swamp Loosestrife)
Hygrophila

SCHEME NO. 2

This is suitable for a tank in an area of less hard water than referred to in Scheme 1.

Fish
5 Tiger Barbs (*Barbus tetrazona*)
5 Cardinal Tetras (*Paracheirodon axelrodi*)
5 Glowlight Tetras (*Hemigrammus erythrozonus*)
2 pairs Guppies (*Poecilia reticulata*)
1 pair Pearl Gourami (*Trichogaster leeri*)
2 Corydoras (*Corydoras aeneus* or *paleatus*)
2 pairs Ruby Barb (*Barbus nigrofasciatus*)
2 small Angelfish (*Petrophyllum scalare*)
5 Zebra Danios (*Brachydanio rerio*)

Plants
Choose from any of the following, plus any from Scheme 1 which, subject to trial and error, thrive in softer water.
Cryptocorynes
Acorus
Cabomba
Ceratopteris

SCHEME NO. 3

Fish
5 Glass Catfish (*Kryptopterus bicirrhis*)
5 Glowlight Tetras (*Hemigrammus erythrozonus*)
1 Siamese Fighting Fish (*Betta splendens*)
2-3 Corydoras (*Corydoras aeneus* or *paleatus*)
1 'Plecostomus' (*Hypostomus sp.*)
3 Harlequins (*Rasbora heteromorpha*)
2 pairs Guppies (*Poecilia reticulata*)
2-3 Clown Loaches (*Botia macracantha*)

Plants
Select any of the plants from Schemes 1 and 2, depending on the hardness of the water. Be prepared for some failures.

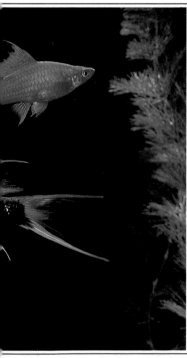

Live-bearing fish make for a colourful aquarium, but don't intermix different fancy strains. Top: Veiltail Guppies (*Poecilia reticulata*); Bottom: two varieties of Swordtail (*Xiphophorus helleri*) – a male Tuxedo Lyre-tail and a female Red Lyre-tail.

Angelfish (*Pterophyllum scalare*)

Ruby Barb (*Barbus nigrofasciatus*)

Cardinal Tetras (*Paracheirodon axelrodi*)

All *Synodontis* catfish have feathery barbels

Peppered Catfish (*Corydoras paleatus*)

Flying Fox (*Epalzeorhyncus kallopterus*)

Aquaria

TANK SIZE
Aquaria come in a wide range of types and designs, to suit all tastes and pockets. They are made in various combinations of materials (Perspex or glass, with or without iron frames). The lightest modern aquaria is made of glass sealed with silicone glue.

Do remember that a tank full of water is very heavy, so it is important to make sure that the bottom of even a lightweight aquarium is fully supported on a firm base.

Unless you need an aquarium for a specialized purpose such as an infirmary or as a rearing or quarantine tank, *never* get one less than 45 cm long, 30 cm wide and 30 cm deep (18 × 12 × 12 in). As a general rule no measurement should ever be less than the depth. Bow-fronted aquaria cost a lot more than the rectangular ones and do little to enhance the quality of life for the fish.

AVOID OVERCROWDING
To work out how many fish may safely be kept in an unaerated tank, the rule is 2.5 cm/1 in of fish body length (excluding tails) for every 75 sq cm/12 sq in of water surface area. For example, a 60 × 30 × 30 cm (24 × 12 × 12 in) tank has a surface area of 1800 sq cm/288 sq in and can accommodate 60 cm/24 in of fish. Tank depth is immaterial in such calculations.

This shoal of Lemon Tetras (*Hyphessobrycon pulchripinnis*) adds the finishing touch to this well-furnished aquarium.

AERATION
Although aeration will greatly increase the tank's fish-holding capacity, do not make its use an excuse to over-stock the tank; suffocation will occur if the aerator fails.

POSITION
It is best to keep an aquarium away from extremes of temperature and also out of continuous bright light, so a window sill is not a good place. Look for a spot away from direct sunlight or a room heater – an alcove beside a chimney breast is often a good place.

A tank 60 cm long and 30 cm wide is a good size for starting off with tropical fish. Although a depth of water of 38 cm makes for a more pleasing 'picture' than 30 cm and gives the fish more swimming room, the deeper tank cannot hold any more fish as the important criterion is the amount of water surface *area*, which remains the same for both tanks.

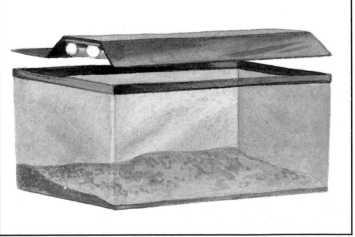

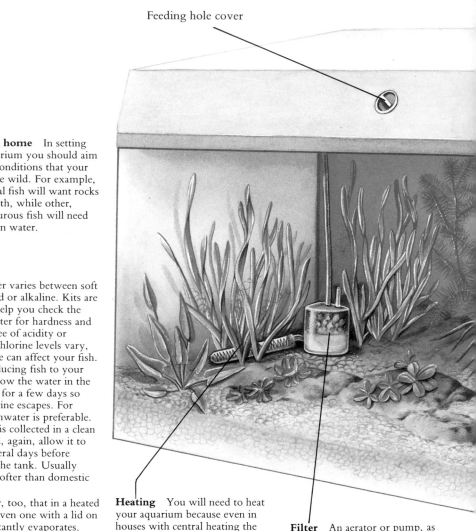

Feeding hole cover

Home from home   In setting up your aquarium you should aim to copy the conditions that your fish like in the wild. For example, shy, nocturnal fish will want rocks to hide beneath, while other, more adventurous fish will need plenty of open water.

Water   Water varies between soft and hard, acid or alkaline. Kits are available to help you check the quality of water for hardness and for pH (degree of acidity or alkalinity). Chlorine levels vary, too, and these can affect your fish. Before introducing fish to your aquarium, allow the water in the tank to stand for a few days so that the chlorine escapes. For some fish rainwater is preferable. Make sure it is collected in a clean container and, again, allow it to stand for several days before putting it in the tank. Usually rainwater is softer than domestic water.

Remember, too, that in a heated aquarium – even one with a lid on – water constantly evaporates. Evaporation will concentrate the minerals in the water and each time you top up, especially with tap water, the mineral concentration will increase. For this reason, regular replacement of, say, 10-15 per cent of water every two or three weeks with previously conditioned water will keep dissolved mineral content down to a safe level. A close-fitting cover-glass will also help to minimize evaporation losses and prevent condensation damage to the aquarium lighting.

Heating   You will need to heat your aquarium because even in houses with central heating the average temperature is too low for most tropical fish. You can buy separate or combined heaters and thermostats. A simple and effective arrangement is to place the heater near the filter or air source, and the thermostat the other side of the tank. The water current will circulate the heat and the thermostat will control it. *Please obey the instructions on wiring up the heater and thermostat very carefully. Water and electricity are a dangerous mixture for both you and the fish.*

Filter   An aerator or pump, as already mentioned, is not essential but is useful, especially if combined with a filter. The filter may be a simple plastic box filled with filter media, through which water is circulated by means of air from the air pump. Detritus is thereby trapped in the filter medium. A useful tip is to place a layer of activated carbon between two layers of filter media, as this will absorb many of the accumulating organic products from fish excretion which can inhibit fish growth.

Ventilated cover A ventilated cover helps to maintain the temperature as well as providing accomodation for lighting. It also helps to keep out dirt, dust and fumes. Fish are susceptible to certain aerosol sprays, so avoid using these in the room where the aquarium is kept.

Lighting For a small aquarium, an ordinary 60 watt bulb may be sufficient for illumination. There are, however, fluorescent tube lights available whose gas content is designed to produce light beneficial to plant growth and to enhance the colours of the fish. Avoid stark bright lights, though, and remember that naturally fish like subdued lighting or shade. Remember, too, that a light bulb, unlike a fluorescent tube light, will increase the water temperature. Fluorescent lights are 'cold' lights.

Thermostat

Thermometer

Aquascaping You will need to put gravel in the bottom of your tank, but please wash it thoroughly first. Put it in a bowl, place this under a running tap and keep stirring the gravel until the water that flows out is quite clear. Rocks are an attractive and useful addition to your aquarium because algae will grow on them and fish can hide beneath them. Do avoid rocks like limestone, though, or those that contain metal ores as these can upset the chemical composition of the water (p.26). Water plants are an essential part of the well-designed aquarium (see pp.30-1). Not only are they visually pleasing, but they also perform several useful functions; they put oxygen into the water; they provide cover for the fish and a surface for egg-laying; and they provide a source of food for some species.

NOTE In this illustration decorative rocks and logs have been omitted so that heaters, thermostats and filters can be seen.

Tank decoration and water quality

ROCKWORK

Apart from adding dramatic interest, rocks can play important roles for the fish and fish keeper alike.

Over a period of time any carefully contoured gravel will tend to flatten out unless it is held up by pieces of rock buried in the gravel. Many fish will retire behind rocks at night-time or when seeking refuge from others; during the day their places will be occupied by nocturnal species, taking their rest during tank-lit hours. Some species will even use rocks and caves as convenient and secure spawning sites.

Rocks should be chosen for their decorative value (interesting strata, or colour) but do not use any soft rocks that are likely to dissolve in the water, nor any with metallic ore veins showing through. Rocks with a high calcium content will harden the water very quickly and should only be used in tanks where species enjoying hard water are to be kept.

For cave-dwelling species, build up caves and grottoes from pieces of rock glued together with a silicone sealant. Always stand large rocks directly on the tank base buried in the gravel; this will avoid any risk of them toppling over on to the fish.

DECORATION

Although there are many air-operated 'action-ornaments' available for the aquarium (and these novelties may well play an important part in attracting youngsters into the hobby), they may not represent quite the ideal tank decoration to the more experienced hobbyist.

Synthetic replicas of logs and branches made from safe resin materials look very realistic – especially when coated with a light layer of natural algae.

A dry diorama of rocks placed behind the aquarium and lit with a low wattage lamp will add 'depth' to the aquarium when viewed from the front. Alternatively, a photographic underwater scene can be fixed to the outside of the aquarium at the back to give a similar effect.

Natural rock

Synthetic log

Synthetic rock

Photo-diorama for fitting around outside of tank

Glass Catfish (*Kryptopterus bicirrhis*)

Siamese Fighting Fish (*Betta splendens*)

WATER QUALITY

As we have seen, everything that is put into the tank will have some effect (both good and bad) upon the water quality. While the newcomer need not worry unduly about actual water conditions (and many hobbyists keep fish in tip-top condition in blissful ignorance of such things), it may be useful to have some basic knowledge of the terms used in defining water quality.

The term pH is used to measure the acidity or alkalinity of the water. Distilled water is neither acidic or alkaline and is referred to as being 'neutral'. The pH scale ranges from 0 to 14 (acid to alkaline) with 7, the midway mark, being the 'neutral' point. As the scale is logarithmic, an increase of 1 in either direction represents a *tenfold* change in conditions.

Water may be soft or hard, depending on the amount of dissolved material in it. Rainwater is soft (the degree of softness depends on how contaminated it becomes as it falls to earth) and is further affected by the type of soil it subsequently flows through or over. Decaying vegetation gives the rain a soft/acid reaction, filtering through calcium-rich earth results in hard/alkaline water.

Domestic water supplies are treated to make them suitable for drinking, not necessarily safe for fish keeping. The removal of chlorine is made easy by the use of dechlorinators available from your aquatic dealer; chlorine can also be removed by vigorous aeration. Treating tap water with a conditioner before using it in a fish tank prevents chemical shocks, often reduces changes in pH and protects the fish's gills.

Aquarium equipment

HEATERS/THERMOSTATS

The normal aquarium heating equipment is the internal type, with the thermostatic unit and heating element enclosed in the same watertight glass tube; temperature adjustment is made by a control protruding through the cap. In large tanks, use two heating units (one at each end) for even distribution of heat. Separate external thermostats, either electro-mechanical or microchip-controlled, can be used with separate heaters if preferred. Allow 10 watts of 'heat' per 5 litres/1 gallon of water: a 150-watt heater will suffice for a 54-litre/12-gallon tank.

AIR PUMPS

Air pumps, in addition to providing aeration (not the necessity some novice fish keepers might think) can be put to other aquarium uses, such as driving filters and aquarium 'vacuum cleaners'. Air pumps should be protected against

This small collection of internal and external equipment is typical of that sufficient for a basic tropical aquarium. The thermometer (1) enables an easy check to be made on the efficiency of the heater/ thermostat unit (2), which is fixed to the aquarium glass with non-toxic clips (3). The air pump (4) delivers air via plastic airline (5) to air stones (6) and the undergravel filter (7) (remember to put this into the tank before the gravel is added!). Algae can be removed from the aquarium glass using the algae-scraper (8). Fluorescent tubes (9) should be replaced regularly.

The aquarium heater can be fixed to the side aquarium glass if preferred. Although a simple internal filter will be adequate for a small aquarium, remember to clean it out regularly, especially when it is out of sight (and maybe out of mind, too) behind a lush growth of plants.

water 'back-siphoning' out of the tank by using a one-way check valve, placed in the airline next to the air pump. Siting the pump above the aquarium is a more obvious answer, but as most fish keepers tend to keep their pump beside or below the aquarium, this protection is vital.

FILTERS

The simplest type of filter is based on a box, filled with various aquarium filter media, through which aquarium water is continuously passed; suspended and dissolved matter is removed by straining or by chemical and adsorptive means. Such filters may be air- or electrically-operated.

Biological filtration units (placed beneath the gravel) effect a waterflow through it, and encourage bacterial colonies to develop which break down toxic waste products.

GRAVEL-WASHERS AND VACUUM CLEANERS

A gravel-washer (a very wide-necked siphoning device) is inserted slightly into the gravel and agitated while water and detritus is removed; the heavier gravel stays behind.

Aquarium 'vacuum-cleaners' are simple airlift devices, raising detritus and water from the aquarium floor and emptying them into a bag where the dirt is collected, the water returning to the tank. Battery-operated versions are available.

Water plants

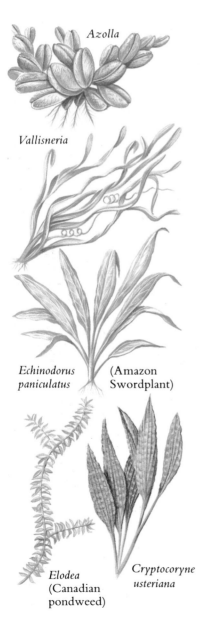

Azolla

Vallisneria

Echinodorus paniculatus

(Amazon Swordplant)

Elodea (Canadian pondweed)

Cryptocoryne usteriana

Water plants are one of the most attractive – and important – aspects of a well-planned aquarium. They come in many sizes and shapes, from bushy growths that hide the corners of the tank, to slender waving fronds that look pretty and give shelter for baby fish. Plants put vital oxygen into the water, too, as well as providing food for some vegetarian fish and hiding places for others. They can also help to reduce algae problems.

Water plants can sometimes be difficult to grow as certain species require specific water conditions and lighting. However, artificial water plants are available and these can provide some greenery in the aquarium until the live plants become established.

For hard water areas *Echinodorus paniculatus* (Amazon Swordplant) is a popular choice. It comes in two varieties, one with narrow and one with broad leaves, and is fairly easy to propagate, too. *Vallisneria* is a slim-leaved plant which is good for producing shade at the back and sides of the tank, and is found in several different varieties. *Elodea* (waterweed or Canadian pondweed) is a rapid grower and provides shade as well as food for some fish. *Sagittaria* with its broad leaves, is another swift-growing plant and a very useful oxygenator.

For areas where the water is softer, try *Cryptocoryne* species. They are excellent foreground plants and very decorative, but tend to be rather slow growers. They vary in size and are good where the light is weak. *Ludwigia* (Swamp Loosestrife) is often a good choice as it grows quickly, is decorative and because its leaves provide useful food. The attractive *Cabomba* is another good oxygenator, useful at the sides and back of the tank.

Most plants, of course, have roots and therefore a suitable coarse sand or gravel (thoroughly washed: see p.25) should be provided for them so that they can grow. Some aquatic plants, however, have a weak root structure and may be sold with a small band of lead (harmless to fish) around their bases to keep them weighted down.

Thickly planted Water Wisteria *(Hygrophila difformis/Synnema triflorum)* provides the backdrop for these Schuberti Barbs.

Despite the beautiful aquarium plants, your attention will be taken most by the red snouts and striped tails of these Rummy-nosed Tetras (*Hemigrammus rhodostomus*).

Fitting out an aquarium

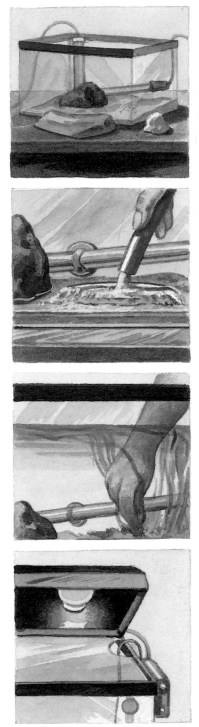

Place the aquarium in position on a **firm, level site**. Sit it on a piece of expanded polystyrene to cushion it against any unevenness on the base surface.

Put undergravel filter in position (if this form of filter is to be used), and add gravel to a sloped depth of 5–8 cm/2–3 in (front to back), using rocks to maintain its contour.

Install thermostat/heater on rear or side glass, clear of the gravel, using non–metallic clips and suction pads. **DO NOT CONNECT TO ELECTRICITY SUPPLY AT THIS STAGE.**

Install filters. Fit airline tube and its anti–siphon valve to air pump and attach other end of airline to input of ganged air–valve; fit airstone to airline (from ganged air–valve output) and place in aquarium or down airlift tube of undergravel filter. Use larger rocks and plants to hide aquarium 'hardware'.

Fill aquarium to within 5 cm/2 in of the top with water. Avoid disturbing the gravel by pouring the water on to a saucer or piece of expanded polystyrene to disperse flow.

Root plants in clumps of gravel: start with rear and sides using tall 'grassy' plants, fill in corners with bushier types. Plant smaller species on open area of gravel near the front glass with single larger plants further back.

Fill tank to final level; place cover–glass, hood and thermometer in position. Cut hood and cover–glass to accommodate tubes and airlines etc where necessary.

Connect wires from lamps, thermostat/heater, filters and air pump to 'cable tidy'. Fit plug and switch on power. Adjust airflow from airstone and water flow from filters as needed. The water will probably reach the required temperature in about a couple of hours.

Home aquarium checklist

1. Talk to expert aquarists and get some ideas.

2. Decide on the site, size, content and cost of your tank.

3. Investigate heating and lighting systems.

4. Purchase tank, stand, cover, heater, thermostat, thermometer, gravel, plants, etc.

5. Thoroughly wash gravel.

6. Clean tank inside and out and put in its permanent site.

7. Place biological (undergravel) filter (if to be used) in tank, fully covering the base. Add gravel.

8. Fix thermostat/heater (following manufacturer's instructions), airstone, internal/external filters (if used) in position.

9. Add rocks and other decorations. Fill tank almost to the top. Add plants and complete aquascaping.

10. Completely fill tank, leaving air space beneath cover-glass. Add thermometer.

11. Connect heating system, air pump and any electrically operated filters to mains. Switch on.

12. Add cover and check lights.

13. Leave tank for at least one week. Make daily temperature checks. Keep an eye out for leaks.

14. Buy your fish. Make absolutely sure the ones you have chosen are compatible with one another.

15. Finally, add your fish to the tank.

Picking out healthy stock

It is extremely important to start off with healthy stock, otherwise your fish will be very short-lived. The standard of supplies of live fish varies enormously, so if possible talk to experienced aquarists and get their advice on who are the best suppliers in your area.

As a general rule, a shop that sells only fish is more likely to be a better choice than one that sells all kinds of pets. The size of the shop is immaterial: some very small establishments may keep fish that are healthier and better-quarantined than much larger places. A shop that specifically states that all its fish are quarantined is better than one that does not. Look especially for tanks labelled 'Not for Sale – Fish in Quarantine'. This means, hopefully, that any diseases imported with the fish will not be present in those finally sold to the customer.

Sometimes, however, in less reputable fish emporia, you may find such notices on some of the aquaria but you may also notice that the water is continually transferring from one tank to the next, thereby transferring any ailments throughout the entire stock of fish. So use your eyes. And take advice.

Once you have chosen your supplier, look at the other inmates of the tanks which contain the fish you want: if there are any unhealthy fish or the tank is very dirty, do not buy, even if your particular choice of fish looks quite unaffected – there is a very real risk you will take disease home with it and so infect your other fish.

A healthy fish will be active (save the nocturnal and naturally sedentary species), with erect fins and smooth skin. Avoid misshapen fish or those which are behaving abnormally.

One final warning: many diseased fish do not show obvious signs of illness, so, especially if you are introducing new fish into an already established aquarium of healthy fish, keep the newcomers separate for a while. Despite all precautions, experience dictates that you should prepare yourself for deaths, although we hope these will be few.

One of the main attractions of fishkeeping is that you can set the levels of attainment yourself. You may be quite content with a simple community collection or you may venture further and maintain a tank of such exotic species as these *Discus*, or Pompadour Fish, which are more suited for the experienced aquarist.

INVESTIGATE BEFORE YOU BUY

Because different species require different conditions, you need to know exactly what you want, and what their requirements are, before you decide which to buy. Moreover, unless you are quite sure you have a male and female of the same species you will never, of course, get them to breed. Information on distinguishing males from females is given on p.44.

It's also important to remember that some fish grow to be much bigger than others (so you will want fewer of them); some large fish will eat smaller ones (quickly reducing your fish population); and the males of certain species will fight endlessly if living together in an aquarium. Some fish prefer to live in small groups, while others are territorial and will threaten the other fish in the tank. Obviously, the larger the aquarium, the greater the number of species of fish you can keep, but don't be tempted to fill your tank with fish which may look good but which won't get on together.

If you are a beginner, it is probably best to start with those fish which are the easiest to keep and the least expensive to buy.

KNOW YOUR FISH FAMILIES

Just to add to the newcomer's confusion, in addition to their classified scientific names, most tropical freshwater fish have common names bestowed upon them by hobbyists and dealers alike. This is all very well, until more than one common name is used for the same species. Different dealers may refer to *Xenocara dolichoptera*, for example as Flag Cat, Blue Chin or Guyanan Blue Fin, which can lead to confusion. Or a common name, such as Red-tailed Black Shark or Chinese Sucking 'Loach', may be deceptive.

By far the best knowledge you can acquire, in respect of fish families, is to know to which group each fish belongs, then you will be in a far better position, first to provide for its needs in the aquarium, and also to understand how it fits in (or not) with other species that you might want to add to your collection.

The challenge of breeding fish will again require you to get to know more about fish families, as not all breed in the same manner; a little advance knowledge is better than hindsight where livestock is concerned. The golden rule is 'always put the fish's interests first'.

The healthy tropical fish

Different species of tropical fish require different conditions, both of temperature and of habitat. However, certain common rules of health apply to them all and it's sensible to observe your fish with these guidelines in mind.

Appetite	good, with food eaten swiftly and with enthusiasm.
Breathing	gill covers rise and fall rhythmically; gulping at the surface (except in the case of labyrinth fish, loaches and some catfish) indicates oxygen starvation.
Demeanour	alert; one fish which leaves the rest of its shoal to be by itself may be sick.
Eyes	usually bright and clear.
Fins	entire, without tears, splits, white spot or streaks of blood; should be held away from the body; not drooping or folded.
Position in water	swimming freely; sick fish may sink to the bottom or float on the surface on their side (although catfish especially often adopt seemingly odd positions).
Scales	scales should show no injury or fungal growth; protruding scales are a sign of disease.
Vent	clean, no trailing faeces.

GENERAL SIGNS OF UNHEALTHINESS

Sunken bellies
Protruding scales
Listlessness (except in some retiring or nocturnal fish)
Discoloured patches on the skin
Ragged fins
White spots
White strands like cottonwool
Milky eyes (where applicable)
Irregular swimming or an irregular position (though some catfish, amongst others, naturally rest at 'peculiar' angles)

Settling in your fish

GETTING THE AQUARIUM READY

Once you have set up your aquarium in its permanent position, planted your plants, and tested out your heating, lighting and filtration system, it is advisable to wait a week or two before you introduce your fish. This gives the plants a chance to get established, enables the water to 'age', and offers you the opportunity to make sure everything is working just as it should.

BRINGING HOME YOUR FISH

Having bought your fish, the next step is to bring them safely home. They will most likely be in plastic bags. If you have a long journey, ask the shop assistant to put the plastic bags in a polystyrene container so that the temperature loss is kept to a minimum. Normally the suplier will ensure that enough air is contained above the water in each bag for the fish to survive; the bag must contain slightly more air than water, and the fish should not be crowded.

INTRODUCING THE FISH TO YOUR AQUARIUM

It is important to remember that fish cannot adapt to sudden changes in temperature, so you need to make sure that the temperature of the water in the plastic bag containing your fish is equal to that in the aquarium. Leave the fish inside the bag in the tank for an hour or two to equalize the water temperatures. Turn the light off, as the bag might touch the bulb and melt, causing problems. When the moment comes for their release, slowly undo or cut the bag and let the fish swim out of their own accord.

You might find it best to keep the light off to begin with while the fish explore their new surroundings, but then turn it on and feed them. Healthy fish enjoy eating, so being given a meal after what has been for them a traumatic experience, can help to settle them down and encourage them to associate their new environment with a regular supply of food.

To transport your fish, place the plastic bag inside a polystyrene container to maintain water temperature.

Feeding

Fish soon learn about food. If you feed them at, say, 7 p.m. each evening, before that time they will be waiting below the spot at which the food is introduced. Regular times for meals are a sensible idea for you and the fish.

A WELL-BALANCED DIET
Most of the proprietary flake foods will be suitable for almost all fish. They have the advantage of containing appropriate amounts of minerals, vitamins, fats and fibres, and are also convenient to dispense. You will need to judge the quantity carefully for yourself, but as a general rule of thumb *don't give fish more food than they can eat in a couple of minutes.* It is better to feed a little and often, rather than too much at one go. Excess food is not always eaten later: it simply pollutes the water and increases the bacteria content and the subsequent risk of disease.

LIVE FOOD IS ALWAYS BENEFICIAL
The most commonly available are small crustaceans called *Daphnia*, or water fleas, which can be put into the tank straight away. You can also get live blood worms (the larvae of mosquito-like insects) and *Tubifex* worms. Be wary of *Tubifex* worms, however, as although they are good and nutritious food, they live half-buried in possibly disease-carrying mud, in foul waters with a low oxygen content.

HOUSEHOLD FOODS CAN BE INCLUDED IN THE MENU
A few ordinary household foods are good for fish, but always give them in *small* quantities mixed with pro-prietary brands. Finely chopped lean meat and ground fish are worth adding to the diet, and so are ground porridge oats and some of the invalid foods. Very small fish (newly born young or dwarf species) will benefit from small quantities of finely crumbled up hard-boiled egg yolks. Vegetarian fish will appreciate small pieces of lettuce leaf.

Water fleas (*Daphnia*)

Tubifex worms   Keep *Tubifex* worms in a bowl under a trickling cold tap for at least three days before you feed them to your fish. Without the mud they knot their bodies into a ball, so you will lose only the dead ones, and the process will rid the rest of any disease they may be carrying.

As an alternative to flake food, tablets of compressed food can be stuck to the aquarium glass for fish to peck at. These young Platies seem to find this one irresistible.

CORRECT FEEDING

Not only is food quantity, quality and size all important but also *how* it is given. Earlier, fish have been described as surface, middle-, or bottom-feeding species and their foods should be presented accordingly. Long-floating flake foods will satisfy surface-feeders but mid- and bottom feeders will need food that sinks more quickly. Nocturnal species, such as catfish, should be fed last thing at night, not merely treated as scavengers and expected to clear up any uneaten food left by other fish.

Maintenance and handling

THE WELL-RUN AQUARIUM

A well-established aquarium will almost run itself, food and light being the only 'fuels' needed to keep it going. One important daily check is to count the fish: notice their condition and be on the look-out for any abnormalities in swimming actions or behaviour. Absentees may be behind rocks or even on the floor! Remove any dead fish to prevent spread of disease.

Scrape off excess algae from time to time, taking care not to scratch the sides of plastic tanks when doing so.

Even the most efficient filter must be periodically cleaned otherwise toxins in the collected detritus may dissolve back into the constantly passing aquarium water.

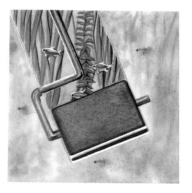

Scraping off excess algae

Fast-growing plants may be pruned back to encourage 'bushing-out' and to provide extra stock. Remove any dead or dying leaves.

The regular removal of, say 10-15 per cent of the water is recommended practice to ensure the mineral content of the water does not become excessively high and also to help cut down the amount of any dissolved waste products: siphoning off the water from the bottom removes detritus in the process. Replace lost water with dechlorinated water of approximately the same temperature.

If a whole strip-down is needed then the first thing to do is **SWITCH OFF THE ELECTRICITY**. Siphon off some aquarium water into a container (a large covered bowl, or spare tank) and, using a net, place the fish into it. Remove the aquarium plants and hardware and place them to one side in a safe place. Siphon out the rest of the water and remove rocks and gravel. **NEVER ATTEMPT TO CARRY THE TANK WITH WATER AND/OR ROCKS AND GRAVEL IN IT**; apart from risking personal injury, it's well-nigh impossible and the bottom glass may easily crack. Rinse gravel clean and scrub rocks. Thoroughly clean out tank with fresh water. Using dechlorinated water if possible, refurnish the tank (as described on p.32); once the water temperature is correct, re-introduce the fish. Clean cover-glass and replace light bulbs or fluorescent light as necessary.

SAFE AND SENSIBLE HANDLING

Fish are delicate and sensitive creatures. Careless handling can easily hurt them, and so can abrupt changes in temperature or light and strong vibrations, like sudden loud noises or tapping on the side of the tank.

In general, fish must not be handled with your bare hands at all, for the reasons explained on p.8. If you must move them to temporary accommodation, it is best to use a net to catch them. In these circumstances, do remember to equalize the water temperature as outlined on p.37.

It is not a good idea to plunge fish abruptly from bright light into sudden darkness or vice versa. If you have a lit aquarium try to remember to turn the light off before the room lights at night, so as to make the transition to darkness gentler and more gradual for the fish.

Should you need to transfer the aquarium to a new home, then try to take as much of the original aquarium water with you as possible; this will lessen the shock to the fish of the transfer. If the journey is long then transport the fish in an insulated container, your dealer may let you have a polystyrene box for this purpose. If the tank is small (up to 60 cm/24 in long), leave the gravel in during transit, but remove rocks, which might topple and break a glass panel.

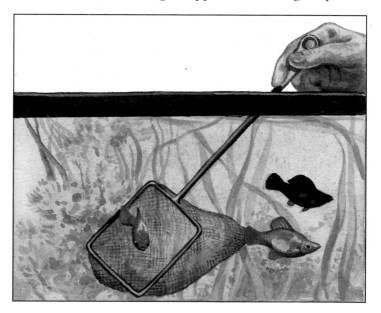

Try to catch fishes as gently as possible when netting. Use a second smaller net to guide the fish into a larger one – this is better than chasing a terrified fish all around the aquarium with a single net.

Ailments

Fish ailments and diseases are very hard to diagnose as superficially similar symptoms may be caused by many different infections. Bacteria, fungi, viruses, protozoa (single-celled organisms) and helminths (internal parasites or worms) can all affect fish. So can adverse environmental factors, over which we may have a certain degree of control.

TOO RAPID TEMPERATURE CHANGE
If a tropical fish is suddenly placed in water that is too cold, it will go into a state of shock (as it will if the heater or thermostat fails). This is manifest in a slow, weaving style of swimming often called shimmying. Too rapid a rise in temperature will cause a shortage of oxygen in the water so that the fish will gasp for breath at the surface.

POISONS
Many of the heavy metals are poisonous to tropical fish. Of these, the worst is copper, so you must avoid having copper in contact with aquarium water. Zinc can also be lethal. Lead, although a poison, is less of a problem (for instance, if used to weight down aquatic plants) because it rapidly becomes covered by a layer of inert lead oxide.

   Other ordinary substances are deleterious to fish health. Aerosol sprays should not be used in close proximity to the aquarium. Insecticides can be lethal.

BAD FEEDING
Complaints due to incorrect feeding may not appear immediately. By the time that something is seen to be wrong, it may be too late. Too much of one type of food can cause intestinal trouble (flake food, however, is mixed) and too much fat and carbohydrate in the diet can lead to degeneration of the digestive organs and the deposition of unhealthy fat. Should your fish persistently have long strings of faeces, something is wrong: try changing the diet, and seek expert advice if things don't improve.

If you have a sick fish, try to isolate it at once, either by putting it in a separate aquarium (a sick tank or infirmary) or by floating a jam jar of aquarium water in the aquarium with the patient therein.

There are some other complaints fish suffer from, which are to some extent outside your control.

WHITE SPOT DISEASE (*Ichthyophthiasis*)

This is a fairly common disease caused by protozoa. The skin of the fish becomes covered by small white spots about the size of a pin head. The damaging organism is called *Ichthyophthirius*, often abbreviated to 'ich'. Ich matures in the skin of the fish where it feeds on skin cells. It then leaves the fish and reproduces. The hundreds of young in their turn feed on the fish, thereby continuing the cycle.

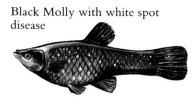

Black Molly with white spot disease

As white spot can only effectively be treated when the parasite is free-swimming, treat the whole aquarium. Quarantining new fish before introducing them to the tank is also very important.

FUNGUS

Fungus is a general term for several different infections that show up as cottonwool-like strands on the fish's body, fins and gills. If left untreated, fungus can be fatal. The spores, which are often present in fish tanks, will attack damaged or sick fish, the fungal growths spreading to vulnerable areas such as eyes and gills. The similar-looking Mouth Fungus is a quite different disease and will not respond to the same treatments, but antibiotics are effective.

BASIC TREATMENT

Isolate any suspect fish as quickly as possible, to avoid the spread of disease. Treatments for white spot, fungus and many other diseases are available from good aquarium shops, but don't expect universal success. There is nothing wrong with many of the medicaments: the problem is that similar symptoms arise from different causes.

There are various chemicals available that can prevent many diseases, but you would be well advised to read widely before using them as, incorrectly applied, they can do more harm than good.

FURTHER ADVICE

Fish-food and accessory manufacturers offer excellent advisory services and answers to many aquatic troubles appear in the 'problem pages' of hobby magazines. If you need urgent help with diagnosing and treating diseases (some spread very quickly), contact your dealer, local aquarist society or a vet specializing in fish.

Reproduction

HOW FISH BREED

All fish develop from eggs but there are two distinct methods of doing so: the majority of fish lay eggs which are fertilized externally, from which the young hatch after a period of hours, days or months depending on the species. Other fish, known as live-bearers, develop internally fertilized eggs within the female's body from where they emerge as free-swimming miniature replicas of their parents.

Live-bearing fish provide the aquarist with the raw material for selective breeding, and this is how all the colourful cultivated strains are made available.

Male live-bearing fish can be identified by their rod-shaped, or notched, anal fin; male fish of egg-laying species are slimmer and much more brightly coloured than females.

BREEDING CONDITIONS

It is very important to realize that different species, as well as being either egg-laying or live-bearing, require different conditions if they are to breed successfully. So, in a mixed tank, the breeding environment that might suit a Guppy can be quite inappropriate for, say, a Gourami.

For example, live-bearing fish young can survive in a heavily weeded community tank without any extra precautions, but egg-laying species require a multitude of different habitats: some scatter their eggs over gravel, into which they fall and subsequently develop unattended by their parents, while others, for example, labyrinth fish such as Gouramis and Siamese Fighting Fish, make bubble nests at the surface and protect them and the young carefully. Some cichlids and catfish lay sticky eggs on to rocks or plants and may or may not (depending on the species), look after the eggs and/or young, while other cichlids excavate nests for their eggs in the sand or gravel.

It is very important to remember that in the wild only a very small proportion of the fry born actually reach adulthood. This is substantially true in home aquarium conditions, too, as many of the young fry are eaten by other fish, including, very often, their own parents. In order to raise the maximum number of young, therefore, it may be necessary to isolate them from the other fish, either by using a separate nursery tank or by putting a divider or partition into your existing aquarium.

FISH BREEDING REQUIRES SPECIALIZED KNOWLEDGE

As you will by now appreciate, tropical fish breeding is a complex business and should not be entered into lightly. If you are intent on breeding your fish, it is strongly recommended that you talk to a number of experienced fish breeders and read a variety of reference books to gain more information and guidance on the subject.

Cichlids guard their young carefully.

Your questions answered

What measures should be taken during power cuts?
The water temperature will fall quite slowly, more so in larger tanks, and a few hours will need to pass before a dangerously low level is reached. If a prolonged power loss is anticipated, particularly in winter months, then the water temperature can be maintained by standing bottles of hot water (heated by alternative means) in the aquarium.

My plants don't appear to grow satisfactorily. How can I get them to thrive?
There are many variables which affect healthy plant growth. These include the amount of light, the depth of gravel and which plants you are growing together. (Like fish, not all plants are compatible, and many houseplants sold as being aquarium-suitable simply aren't!)
   Another reason may be the use of undergravel filters but this is a very contentious point amongst aquarists.

How can I tell whether my fish are males or females?
Most male live-bearers have a rod-shaped anal fin; females have the normal fan-shaped fin. Males of egg-laying species are slimmer, more brightly coloured and have longer fins than the females, which are plumper, a condition more easily seen from above.

Why are partial water changes necessary if a filter is fitted?
Not all filters remove dissolved water products totally. Changing a proportion of aquarium water regularly helps to keep down the levels of dissolved wastes and ensures that trace elements are kept at optimum levels.

My catfish often dash to the surface and gulp air. Is the aquarium lacking in oxygen?
No. Catfish use air gulped at the surface as an alternative to breathing dissolved oxygen; it is absorbed into their blood in a special section in their gut.

How should fish be looked after in my absence?

Healthy, well-fed fish can generally be left to their own devices for up to two weeks. Giving a non-fishkeeping neighbour the task of feeding them may result in over-feeding unless small pre-packed 'meals' are left, with *very strict* instructions on how to feed them. Alternatively, you can purchase a 'vacation feeder', which releases small food particles over a period of time. However, a responsible person should be asked to check the tank daily to ensure that electrical equipment is working properly.

How often should I clean out the filter?

It all depends on how dirty the aquarium is; rinsing the filter medium (in *aquarium water*) every two–three weeks will lengthen its life for a while; any lessening waterflow from filters indicates that cleaning out has been left too late!

My fish have begun to hang at the surface, gasping for air. What is wrong?

They are indicating that there is insufficient oxygen in the water or that they cannot make use of what is available. Increase aeration (the pump may have stopped, the tank may be overcrowded or there may be a lot of decaying matter on the tank floor), and check for inflamed gills and increased breathing rates. The latter may be due to a parasitic infection of the gills: seek qualified help.

Why do my fish scratch about on the rocks?

They may be infested with a skin parasite which they are attempting to dislodge by their scratching actions. Seek advice from an experienced aquarist, vet or your dealer for accurate diagnosis. The condition is quite curable.

Shortly after setting up my aquarium, the water turned misty. Will it clear or should I start again?

You should remember that the aquarium is a collection of many living things, not just the fish and plants. There is quite likely to be a rapid development of bacteria and minute algae spores in the water that will produce such an effect until the plants become established and the aquarium reaches some point of natural balance. Modern filters will help to keep cloudiness at bay (it may only be dirt stirred up by fish, after all) and so can you by carrying out regular partial water changes and never overfeeding, as any 'left-overs' will contribute to water pollution.

Index

Acorus, 19
Aeration, 22, 27, 28-9
Ailments, 34, 42-3, 47
Air pump, 28
Algae, 28, 30, 40, 47
Amazon Swordplant, 18, 30
Angelfish, 6, 10, 14, 18, 19, 20
Aquaria, 18, 22-9, 32-3, 37, 40-1
Aquascaping, 25, 26, 32, 33
Azolla, 30

Barbels, 9, 16
Barbs, 6, 10
Barbus nigrofasciatus. See Ruby Barb
Barbus tetrazona. See Tiger Barb
Betta splendens. See Siamese Fighting Fish
Biology, 8-9
Botia macracantha. See Clown Loach
Bottom dwellers, 10, 39
Brachydanio rerio. See Zebra Danio
Breathing, 26
Breeding, 10, 11, 12, 14, 15, 44-5
Bronze Catfish, 16
Butterfly Fish, 13

Cabomba, 19, 20
Canadian pondweed, 30
Cardinal Tetra, 6, 14, 19, 20
Catfish, 6, 9, 10, 16, 21, 36, 39, 44, 46
See also Bronze, Peppered *and* Pleco
Ceratopteris, 19
Characin, 9
Chinese Sucking 'Loach', 16, 35
Choosing fish, 10, 34-5
Cichlids, 6, 26, 44, 45
Clown Loach, 17, 19
Compatability, 10, 18-19, 35

Corydoras, 6, 18, 19
Corydoras aeneus. See Bronze Catfish
Corydoras paleatus. See Peppered Catfish
Cryptocorynes, 19, 30

Danio, 10
Daphnia, 15, 38
Diorama, 26
Discus, 34

Echinodorus paniculatus. See Amazon Swordplant
Egg-layers, 12, 13, 14-15, 16-17, 44-5
Eggs, 25, 44
Elodea. See Canadian pondweed
Epalzeorhynchus kallopterus. See Flying Fox
Eyes, 8, 36

Feeding, 37, 38-9, 42, 47
Filter, 24, 29, 32, 33, 40, 46, 47
Fins, 8-9, 36
'Fish capacity', 22
Fish families, 35
Flying Fox, 21
Fungus, 43

Gasteropelecus sternicla. See Silver Hatchetfish
Gills, 8, 47
Glass Catfish, 12, 19, 27
Glowlight Tetra, 14, 19
Gourami, 6, 10, 44
See also Pearl
Gravel washer, 29
Guppy, 6, 10, 18, 19, 44
Gyrinocheilus aymonieri. See Chinese Sucking 'Loach'

Handling, 8, 41
Harlequins, 15, 19
Health, 34, 36
Heating, 24, 28, 32, 33
Hemigrammus erythrozonus. See Glowlight Tetra
Hygrophila, 18
Hypostomus plecostomus. See 'Pleco'

Ichthyophthiriasis. See White spot disease

Killifish, 6
Kryptopterus bicirrhis. See Glass Catfish

Labeo bicolor. See Red-tailed Black Shark
Labyrinth fish, 44
Lateral line, 9
Lighting, 25
Live-bearers, 10-11, 44-5
Loach, 9
Logs, 26
Ludwigia. See Swamp Loosestrife

Maintenance, 40-1
Midwater feeders, 14-15, 39
Molly, 6, 10, 18
Mouth fungus, 43
Muscle segment, 5

Native habits, 6-7
Neon Tetra, 6
Nursery tank, 45

Operculum (gill cover), 8

Pantadon buchholzi. See Butterfly Fish
Paracheirodon axelrodi. See Cardinal Tetra
Pearl Gourami, 15, 18, 19
Peppered Catfish, 16, 21
Platy, 6, 10, 11, 18
'Pleco', 17, 19
Poecilia reticulata. See Guppy
Poecilia spp. *See* Molly
Poisons, 42
Pterophyllum scalare. See Angelfish

Quarantine, 22, 34

Rasbora hetermorpha. See Harlequin
Rasboras, 6, 10
Red-tailed Black Shark, 35
Reproduction, 44-5
Rocks, 26, 32, 33
Ruby Barb, 15, 19, 20

Sagittaria, 18, 30
Scales, 8, 36
Sexing, 44, 46
Siamese Fighting Fish, 6, 12, 19, 27, 44
Silver Hatchetfish, 12
Suckermouth Catfish. *See* 'Pleco'
Surface feeders, 12-13, 39
Swamp Loosestrife, 18, 30
Swim bladder, 9

Swordtail, 6, 9, 10, 18

Tail (caudal) fin, 9
Temperature, 11, 12, 32, 41, 46
Tetra, 10 *See also* Glowlight, Neon *and* Cardinal
Thermometer, 25, 28, 33
Thermostat, 24, 32, 33
Tiger Barb, 15, 18, 19
Transporting fish, 37, 41
Trichogaster leeri. See Pearl Gourami
Tubifex worms, 38

Vacuum cleaners, 28, 29
Vallisneria, 18, 30
Vent, 36
Ventilation, 25

Water, 18, 19, 24, 27, 40, 47
Water fleas. *See Daphia*
Water plants, 25, 30-1, 32, 33, 37, 40, 46
White spot disease, 43

Xenocara dolichoptera, 35
Xiphophorus helleri. See Swordtail
Xiphophorus maculatus. See Platy

Zebra Danio, 12, 19